FIFE COUNCIL LIBRARIES

D1080120

CHILDREN IN HISTORY
The 60s & 70s

Kate Jackson Bedford

W

FRANKLIN WATTS
LONDON • SYDNEY

First published in 2009 by
Franklin Watts
338 Euston Road
London NW1 3BH

Franklin Watts Australia
Hachette Children's Books
Level 17/207 Kent Street
Sydney NSW 2000

Copyright © Franklin Watts 2009

ISBN 978 0 7496 8701 4

Dewey classification: 941.085'6

Series editor: Jeremy Smith
Art director: Jonathan Hair
Design: Jane Hawkins
Cover design: Jane Hawkins
Picture research: Diana Morris

Picture credits: Advertising Archives: 10t, 10b, 11t, 11b, 16c, 24b. Sam Appleby/Photofusion/Alamy: 8b. Arcaid/Corbis: 9. Anthony Berenyi/istockphoto: 20c. Bandphoto/UPPA/Topfoto: 26b. Classic Stock/Topfoto: 6t, 6b, 30b. Mary Evans Picture Library: 5b, 7, 12t, 12c, 12b, 13, 14b. Eyewave/istockphoto: 10c. Greenpeace: 5t. Brian Harris/Alamy: 4c. Hulton Archive/Getty Images: 4t, 4b. Interfoto Pressbild/Alamy: 20t, 20b. Colin Jones/Topfoto: front cover b, 27b. John Lamb/Stone/Getty Images: front cover tl. Ray Lancaster/Hulton Archive/Getty Images: 14t, 14c. Land of Lost Content/HIP/Topfoto: 18b, 24t, 24c, 25. Lucas Film/20th Century Fox/Kobal Collection: 28t, 29. Roger Mayne/Mary Evans Picture Library: 8t, 8c, 30t. Erin Moloney/Topfoto: 18t, 19. NASA: 26t, 26c, 30ca. Picturepoint/Topham: 22c.

Picture Post/Hulton Archive/Getty Images: 16t, 16b. H. Armstrong Roberts/Alamy: 6c. Science Museum/Science & Society Picture Library: front cover tc, 17b, 21. Shinypix/Alamy: 23b. Hugh Trefall/Alamy; 2, 22t, 23t. Topfoto: 1, 15, 22b, 30cb. Nick Wheeler/Corbis: 18c. Ethel Wolvovitz/Image Works/ Topfoto: 28b.

Every attempt has been made to clear copyright. Should there be any inadvertent omission please apply to the publisher for rectification.

A CIP catalogue record for this book is available from the British Library

Printed in China

FIFE COUNCIL SCHOOLS	
921322	
PETERS	12-Oct-2009
J941.085	£12.99
JPAS	AD

Contents

Swinging times   4

Family life   6

At home   8

Meal times   10

Going to school   12

What to wear   14

Toys and games   16

Being entertained   18

High tech   20

Television and music   22

On holiday   24

Memorable events   26

Activities   28

Timeline   30

Glossary and further information   31

Index   32

Swinging times

At the beginning of the 1960s, children and their parents lived their lives in a traditional way. As the next twenty years progressed this changed, and children started to experience different childhoods from their parents.

Swinging sixties

In the 60s, many young people had different ideas about life compared with their parents and older generations. They dressed differently and followed new trends in music. Young people tried to change things in the world by protesting about social problems and wars.

▲ Rubbish piled up in the streets during the winter of 1979 because the workers who usually collected it were on strike.

Strange seventies

Britain had many problems in the 70s. The cost of living for families rose as the price of goods like food and petrol went up. A miner's strike in 1973 led to a shortage of coal for power stations, causing power cuts. The government brought in a three-day working week to save energy.

▲ These young people are enjoying a music festival in the late 60s.

Caring for the environment

During the 1970s people became more aware of how important it is to care for the environment. The World Wildlife Fund showed how many animals were at risk of extinction and worked to help protect animals and their habitats. Discoveries, such as the harmful effects on the ozone layer of CFCs from aerosols and fridges, made people realise how easily the Earth can be damaged.

◀ The organisation, Greenpeace, used their ship, *Rainbow Warrior* (left), to take action against people who were harming the environment.

Children's lives

Children growing up in the 60s and 70s, less than 50 years ago, had a different childhood compared with today. Their lives were simpler, with less technology. There were no mobile phones and few computers. However, during the two decades, family life did begin to change.

▶ These children are playing a swinging game around a lamppost in the 1970s.

Family life

In the 60s and 70s, most families were made up of two married parents and two or three children. Families often lived further away from grandparents than in previous generations. They had moved away from home to find work.

Family roles

Most mothers and fathers followed traditional roles. Young children were looked after by their mother at home, while the father went out to work. Mothers also took care of the house, doing all the housework and cooking which took up more time than they do today.

▲ Children spent most of their time with their mother.

Changing families

Family life changed for some children after new divorce laws were made in the 70s. Until then, most couples stayed married for life and children lived with both parents. Gradually it became more common for families to split up and children to live with one parent, often their mother, and only see their father at weekends.

▲ New electrical gadgets, like this food mixer, helped to make household jobs quicker and easier.

A new country

Many families came to live in Britain during the 60s and 70s, from countries such as Pakistan and the Caribbean. Newly-arrived children had to start a new school, sometimes learn a new language and get used to the different way of life and weather in Britain.

▼ These children's parents came to Britain from the Caribbean.

Starting again

In 1972, thousands of Asian children and their parents fled to Britain from Uganda in East Africa. The ruler of Uganda, Idi Amin, suddenly ordered all Asians with British passports to leave the country in 48 hours. They weren't allowed to take much money or many possessions with them. When they arrived in Britain they had to start all over again, finding new homes, jobs and schools.

At home

Many children moved into newly-built homes in the 60s and 70s. Some families moved out from city centres to new homes built on the edge of towns, or to one of the new towns being built throughout Britain.

Few home comforts

In the 60s, some children still lived in homes without indoor bathrooms or toilets. They washed in a tin bath in front of a coal fire in the living room. Many families didn't have a washing machine so the mother had to wash clothes by hand. Those who did have a washing machine, often had a twin tub.

▶ These children from the 1960s are having their bath in the living room.

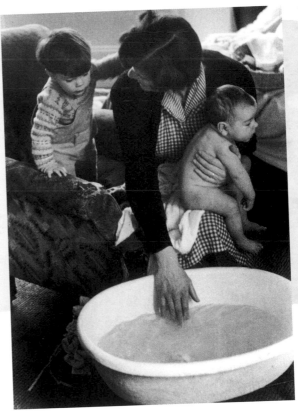

▲ The council-owned Stonebridge Estate in north-west London.

New council home

Thousands of families began living in newly-built council homes. For many children this was the first time they had lived in a house with an indoor bathroom. Even so, some of the new homes were heated by coal fires downstairs so bedrooms were often cold in winter. Children sometimes woke up to find frost on the inside of their bedroom window.

▶ This huge tower block was home to many children.

High rise

New concrete tower blocks of flats became home to many children and their families in the 60s. They moved into the new flats from areas of poor housing in the cities. Children who lived in the new tower blocks often had no garden to play in and had to reach their flat using a lift or stairs.

Seventies style

Orange and brown were popular colours for decorating homes in the 70s. Brown paint, dark wood and orange and brown patterns covered many surfaces. White bathroom fittings were replaced with baths in new colours, such as avocado and aubergine, named after the foods that more people were discovering.

Meal times

Most of the meals children ate in the early-60s were cooked at home from scratch, using basic ingredients. The types of fruit and vegetables eaten depended on the season. Children only ate fruits, such as strawberries, when they were available in the summer.

New tastes

Children's diets started to change when their parents began to cook new recipes with ingredients brought in from other countries. Families were introduced to new tastes on holidays abroad, or by people who had moved to Britain from countries such as India, Asia or the Caribbean.

▲ Children tried exotic foods, including the avocado pear, for the first time.

Quick and easy

New foods that were convenient, quick and easy to prepare became part of many children's diets in the '70s. An instant pudding called Angel Delight, made by adding milk to a powder, was very popular with children. Some families bought a freezer and ate frozen foods, such as Findus crispy pancakes and Arctic rolls.

◄ An Arctic roll was ice cream, wrapped in a layer of sponge cake. Many children loved it.

THE BIRDS EYE GUIDE TO BETTER EATING

Perfect Marriage

ARCTIC ROLL is the result of a perfect marriage arranged by Birds Eye. We have joined together two favourite sweets —light-as-air sponge, and smooth, rich ice cream. Each is delicious on its own, but perfection when eaten together. And both are quick-frozen the Birds Eye way so they taste as fresh as the moment they were made. A wonderful dessert for any meal, and extra-specially good with fruit like these Birds Eye strawberries.

Arctic Roll is just one of the many fine things to eat in the Birds Eye range of quality foods. No wonder you eat better with Birds Eye.

Eat Better with

Smash potato

Television adverts tell us what kind of foods were popular at a particular time. Smash was an instant mash potato, popular with many children in the 70s. Adverts showed aliens from Mars who laughed at the idea of digging up potatoes from the ground, peeling them, cooking and mashing them. Making Smash was much quicker and easier.

▶ The Smash adverts, using tin aliens from Mars, helped to make Smash a popular food in school canteens and at home.

Buying food

Families began to do lots of their shopping in supermarkets. Unlike a traditional grocer's shop, where customers were served by the shopkeeper, people helped themselves in supermarkets. Prices were cheaper in supermarkets and there was a much wider choice of foods. Children also ate take-away meals bought from the newly-opened McDonalds, as well as Chinese and Indian take-aways.

◀ The first McDonalds in Britain opened in Woolwich in 1974.

Going to school

Going to school was part of normal life for children in the 60s and 70s. In class they often sat in groups around a large table. Lessons included English, maths and topic work about different subjects.

Milk time

Throughout the 60s and early-70s, all primary school children were given a free third of a pint of milk a day at school. In 1971 Margaret Thatcher, a government minister, stopped free milk for children over seven years old. She was known as 'Thatcher, Thatcher, milk snatcher', and later she became the first woman Prime Minister.

▶ Children drank their milk by piercing the foil milk bottle top with a straw.

Well behaved

Children were expected to respect their teachers and be well behaved at school. In grammar schools, children stood up when their teacher entered the classroom. Teachers were allowed to punish naughty children with a smack from a slipper, a ruler or a cane.

◀ These grammar school children were expected to work hard at school.

Going comprehensive

When children were in their last year of primary school they took an exam called the 11+, to decide which school they went to next. Children who passed the 11+ went to a grammar school, those who failed went to a secondary modern. During the 70s, this system began to change and most children attended comprehensive schools.

School uniform

Not all children wore a school uniform in the 60s and 70s. Many children went to primary school in their everyday clothes. Uniforms were worn at grammar and secondary schools. Often there were strict rules about uniform. The length of a girl's skirt was sometimes checked with a ruler to make sure it wasn't too short.

► Most secondary school uniforms included a school blazer, like this one from the 70s.

13

What to wear

In the early 60s, children wore clothes that were smaller versions of adult clothes. As fashions changed, children's clothes followed the new trends and looked different and were more casual, comfortable and bright.

Sixties style

Most boys in the 60s still wore traditional clothes. They dressed in shorts until they went to secondary school when they changed to wearing long trousers. Girls wore dresses, skirts and jumpers. The length of their skirts followed the changing fashions and became shorter, ending above the knee.

▲ Most people wore wide, flared trousers in the 70s.

No taste

The 70s became known as 'the decade that taste forgot' because the fashions were so different and brightly coloured. Children's clothes followed similar fashions to adult clothes. Boys and girls wore long trousers with wide, flared bottoms. Jeans, cheesecloth shirts and a style of jumper without sleeves, known as a tank top, were popular.

▲ These young people are wearing typical 1960s clothes.

Looking casual

Many children and adults wear jeans today because of a trend started in the '60s. Until then, jeans were only worn by workers who did factory or labouring jobs. In the '60s jeans became popular with young people because they looked casual, were comfortable, hard-wearing and it was impossible to tell how rich or poor a person was.

From head to foot

Children's hairstyles changed in the '70s. Boys grew their hair longer and many girls had a short pageboy style. In the 60s, most children wore sensible T-bar shoes, but in the 70s children's shoes became more fashionable. Children wore shoes with big, chunky heels that were smaller versions of the high-heeled platform shoes that were worn by adults.

▼ Some of these boys have longer hairstyles, fashionable in the 1970s.

Toys and games

Children had more freedom than today and spent lots of time playing outside in the 60s and 70s. There were fewer cars in the streets and neighbours kept an eye on each other's children to make sure they were safe.

Playtime

At break times, school children played lots of outdoor games including football, cricket, skipping, hopscotch, balancing on stilts and bouncing on pogo sticks. Many children threw a ball against a wall as they sang rhymes.

▲ Children drew pictures on etch-a-sketch by turning the two knobs.

Indoor toys

Many girls played with Barbie or Sindy dolls, which they dressed in fashionable clothes. Boys played with Action Man dolls. Drawing toys, such as spirograph and etch-a-sketch, were popular. Families played board games, including Monopoly and Cluedo.

▲ These children are playing a skipping game in the 60s.

Jumping

One of the toys most children wanted in the 70s was a space hopper. They were large, orange, air-filled balls made from rubber, with a smiley face on the front and two horn-like ears. Children sat on them, held onto the horns and jumped about. Some children raced each other on their space hoppers.

▶ A bright orange space hoppers from the 70s.

Getting around

In the 70s, many children rode a new style of bike called a Chopper. It had a long L-shaped seat, a gear stick, long bent-back handle bars and a smaller wheel at the front. Younger children had a bike called a Chipper. It was similar to a Chopper, but it had no gears. Skateboards also became popular and children learnt to do stunts on them.

▼ Chopper bikes were fashionable in the 70s.

Being entertained

Children didn't have computer games, or much choice of television programmes to watch in the 60s. They had fun playing with toys and games and spent time outside with their friends.

In a pack

Many children belonged to a pack of Brownies, Guides, Cubs or Scouts. Every week, they met to play games, build a camp fire or learn useful skills, such as first aid or how to cycle safely. Children earned badges to sew onto their uniform.

▶ This girl from the 70s is wearing her Brownie uniform.

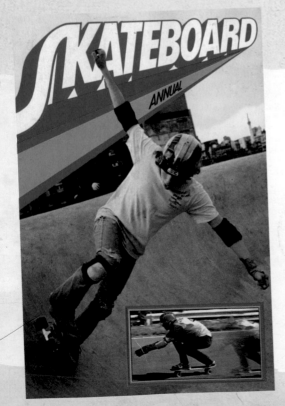

Reading time

With less television to watch and no computer games to play, children found other things to do, including reading. Comics such as the *Beano*, *Dandy*, *Marvel* and *Batman* were popular with boys. Girls enjoyed *Judy*, *Girl* and *Mandy*. Most children enjoyed Enid Blyton adventure stories, as well as books by many other authors.

◀ Skateboarding was so popular that there was even a comic devoted to it.

Films

In the 70s, blockbuster films aimed at both children and adults, arrived in Britain. *Jaws (1975)*, a film about a man-eating great white shark, scared millions of people. In 1977, the first *Star Wars* film was released. It broke records as people flocked to the cinema.

▶ Star Wars toys helped children act out their own light sabre battles.

60S AND 70S LEGACY

Film toys

The first ever children's toys from a film were made for *Star Wars* in 1977. Children collected toy figures of the characters and models of the space ships and acted out their own version of the adventures. Today, there are many children's toys linked to films and TV shows.

High tech

In the 70s, children began to use the new electrical gadgets that became available. The huge advances in technology in the 60s and 70s led to many new inventions.

Getting smaller

Children did not use computers in the 60s. The only computers at that time were large and expensive machines used by governments and businesses. The invention of the silicon chip changed technology and made it possible to make smaller electrical gadgets. By the late-70s some children were playing games on the new small personal computers.

▲ A family play the Odyssey 2001 computer game at home in 1978.

▶ A digital watch from the late '70s.

On time

Digital watches were worn by many children when they became popular in the 70s. The watches used the new LCD — liquid crystal display — and showed the time in digital figures. Children could even read the time in the dark by pressing a button to light up the time display. Some digital watches had stopwatches and an alarm.

Video game

The first video game children played was invented in 1972 in the USA. It was a simple game called Pong, based on ping-pong or table tennis. Children played it by batting a spot of light back and forth across the screen. Pong was popular in arcades and children played a smaller version that plugged into a television set at home.

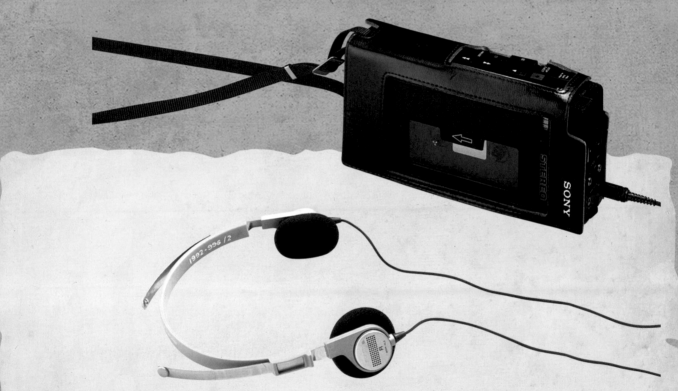

On the move

In the late-70s, children started listening to music while they were on the move with the new Sony Walkman. It was a small portable cassette player that was clipped onto a belt or fitted into a pocket, and had headphones to listen to the music. Many children used their Walkmans on car or train journeys.

▲ Walkmans made it easy for children to listen to music anywhere.

Television and music

Children growing up in the 60s watched less television than today. Some families did not have a television. There were few channels to choose from, and the picture was black and white until 1967.

Children's TV

Only a few children's programmes were broadcast in the early-60s, usually one after lunch and another later in the afternoon. Gradually the number of children's programmes increased. Children watched them when they got home from school. Children's favourites included Blue Peter, Rentaghost and the Magic Roundabout.

▲ Animal Magic was a popular children's show that looked at the world of animals.

▲ The Bay City Rollers pop group came from Scotland.

Pop music

Many children enjoyed pop music. Bands like the Beatles, Monkees, Osmonds and Bay City Rollers were popular. Children listened to pop music on vinyl records on a record player. Some children even copied their favourite band's style of clothes.

Doctor Who

Doctor Who, one of the most popular TV programmes with children today, started in November 1963. In the first episode, Doctor Who and the Tardis, disguised as a police call box, were discovered in a junkyard in London. Since then there have been 10 'Doctors' who have fought with many different monsters throughout time and space.

▶The Daleks are one of the Doctor's greatest enemies.

▼ These portable cassette players ran on batteries or could be plugged into the mains.

On tape

Children started listening to music on tape in the 70s, using the new portable cassette recorders. Children also recorded their own music tapes using cassette recorders. When video recorders first became available at the end of the 70s, children could watch their favourite television programmes again and again.

On holiday

The way children and their parents spent their holidays began to change during the 60s and 70s. Families had more money to spend and some spent it enjoying holidays away from home.

Seaside holidays

Some children spent their holidays camping or staying in a rented caravan in different parts of Britain. It became easier and quicker for families to travel because they could drive on the newly-built motorways. Staying near the sea was popular with children — they enjoyed building sandcastles and playing in the sea, just as they do today.

▲ This family have set up their camper van at the seaside.

Holiday camps

Thousands of children went to popular holiday camps. Butlin's camps were at places on the coast, such as Skegness, Filey and Minehead. Each camp was a self-contained village where families stayed in chalets. All the meals, entertainment and sport was organised for them.

◄ Adverts encouraged families to spend their holidays at Butlin's.

Butlin's fun

Children enjoyed holidays at Butlin's because there was so much to do in a safe, friendly environment. While they were on holiday, children swam in the camp swimming pool, had fun on the rides in the amusement parks, played in the playgrounds and took part in the sports events. Places like Butlins continue to attract thousands of visitors today.

Going abroad

More families started to travel abroad for their holiday, instead of staying in Britain. Children went with their parents on package holidays and flew to places such as the Costa Brava in Spain or Greece, where there was beautiful weather and warm seas.

▶ Foreign holidays, with good weather, tempted many people to travel abroad.

HOLIDAY **Fanfare** 1/6 1963

Where to go ★ How to get there ★ What it costs **WIN £150 HOLIDAY**

Memorable events

The children who grew up in the 60s and 70s witnessed many unforgettable events. These included the assassination of President Kennedy in 1963 and the Moon landing in 1969.

Aberfan disaster

One hundred and sixteen children and twenty-eight adults were killed in a terrible disaster in 1966. At 9.15 am on 21st October, a huge heap of coal waste slid down into the village of Aberfan in Wales. It swept away trees and cottages and buried the village primary school.

▲ Rescuers searched desperately for any survivors in the Aberfan school.

▲ Neil Armstrong, the first man to walk on the Moon.

Man on the Moon

On 21st July 1969, people all over the world watched on television as the first man walked on the Moon. When American astronaut, Neil Armstrong, stepped onto the Moon he said the famous words, "That's one small step for man, one giant leap for mankind."

Going decimal

British children and adults had to start using a new system of currency in 1971. On 15th February, Britain stopped using the traditional currency of 12 pennies to a shilling, and twenty shillings to a pound and switched to decimal currency, like other European countries. The new currency of 100 new pennies to one pound was much simpler.

Queen's Silver Jubilee

In 1977, Queen Elizabeth II celebrated 25 years on the throne. Children all over Britain took part in events to celebrate this Silver Jubilee. Many children went to big outdoor street parties where they had a tea of sandwiches, jelly, ice-cream and cake. Some children received commemorative mugs and coins to keep.

▼ These children are enjoying a Silver Jubilee street party.

Activities

Why not experience some of the '60s and '70s by trying some of these activities?

Hula hoop

A popular game in the 60s used a large plastic hoop called a hula hoop, named after the Hawaiian Hula dance. The aim of the game is to spin the hula around your waist and keep it moving around for as long as possible by wriggling your body from side to side inside the hoop.

60s and 70s food

Try some of the instant foods that were popular at this time, and which are still available today: Angel Delight, Artic roll, Findus crispy pancakes, pot noodles and sandwich spread.

Many people tried cheese fondue for the first time in the 70s — try this recipe for yourself.

ASK AN ADULT TO HELP YOU MAKE THE FONDU. NEVER USE A COOKER WITHOUT ADULT HELP.

Ingredients:

- 475 ml milk
- 6 g mustard powder
- 1 clove garlic, peeled and crushed
- 25 g cornflour
- 680 g shredded Cheddar cheese, or a mixture of your favourite cheeses
- black pepper
- vegetable sticks, bread sticks, cubes of bread

Mix together the milk, mustard powder, garlic and flour in a saucepan. Heat until almost boiling. Gradually stir in the cheese and wait until all the cheese has melted. Season with black pepper and eat immediately. You do this by dipping raw vegetable sticks, bread sticks or cubes of bread into the cheese fondu.

Get reading

Read some of these children's books and comics from the 60s and 70s:

- *Stig of the Dump* – Clive King,

- *James and the Giant Peach* or *Charlie and the Chocolate Factory* – Roald Dahl,

- *Lizzie Dripping* – Helen Cresswell,

- *The Peppermint Pig* – Nina Bawden,

- *Famous Five* adventures – Enid Blyton,

- The *Beano* or *Dandy*.

Watch a film

Try watching some of the films that were popular with children in the 60s and 70s:

- *The Sound of Music*,

- *Chitty, Chitty, Bang, Bang*,

- *Jungle Book*,

- *Star Wars* – Episode IV,

- *Jaws*,

- *Mary Poppins*,

- *Bednobs and Broomsticks*.

Timeline

1960 President John F Kennedy elected President of USA.

1961 Russia sends the first man into space.

1962 The Beatles have their first hit record.

1963 US President Kennedy is assassinated.

1963 First episode of Doctor Who is shown on television.

1965 Women start to wear mini skirts.

1966 England wins the football World Cup.

1966 The Aberfan disaster kills 116 children.

1969 First men walk on the Moon.

1969 Concorde — the supersonic airliner makes its first flight.

1971 Free school milk for children over the age of seven is abolished.

1971 Decimal currency is introduced.

1972 First pocket calculator is invented.

1973 The miner's strike leads to a shortage of coal.

1974 Government introduces three-day working week to save electricity. Power cuts affect everyone.

1975 The film *Jaws* scares people in the cinema.

1976 Concorde starts carrying passengers from London to Paris.

1976 A heatwave in Britain — the hottest weather for 200 years.

1977 Queen's Silver Jubilee — celebrations all over Britain.

1977 Millions of people flock to see *Star Wars*.

1978 The first test-tube baby is born.

1979 Winter of discontent. Workers strike and the streets fill up with rubbish.

1979 First female British Prime Minister, Margaret Thatcher, is elected.

Glossary and further information

Assassination A murder for political or religious reasons.

CFCs The shortened name of chemical compounds called chlorofluorocarbons, used as propellants in aerosol cans.

Chalets Small houses families stayed in at holiday camps.

Currency The money used in a country, such as pounds and pence.

Divorce A legal end to a marriage.

Ozone layer A layer in the Earth's atmosphere which protects life on Earth from the Sun's damaging ultraviolet light.

Package holiday Holidays where all the arrangements are made by the tour company.

Pogo stick A toy that looked like a stilt with two foot rests and handlebars. Children stood on them and bounced up and down.

Police call box A special type of telephone box used by policemen to contact the police station before they had radios.

Silicon chip Small electronic circuits used in electronic equipment such as computers.

Slums Poor, dirty, overcrowded housing.

Strike Workers stop working because of a quarrel with their employers over wages or other problems.

Finding out more about life in the 60s and 70s

Your parents, grandparents and teachers may have grown up in the 60s and 70s and can tell you what life was like for them. Look at photographs of them when they were children and ask them about the games they played, the clothes they wore, what they liked watching on television and what was their favourite food.

There are museums and websites you can visit to find out more about how children lived in the 60s and 70s.

www.learningcurve.gov.uk Find out about people who moved to Britain in the 60s and 70s.

www.vam.ac.uk/moc/index.html The V&A Museum of Childhood in London has displays of children's toys and games from the 60s and 70s.

http://news.bbc.co.uk/1/hi/magazine/6707679.stm Read people's memories of life in Britain during the 60s.

http://news.bbc.co.uk/1/hi/magazine/6729701.stm Memories of life in 70s Britain.

Index

Aberfan disaster 26, 30
adverts 11, 24, 25
Armstrong, Neil 26

books 18, 29
Butlin's 24, 25

Caribbean 7, 10
cassette player/recorder 21, 23
Choppers 17
clothes 4, 13, 14-15, 16, 22
comics 18, 29
computers 5, 18, 20

decimal currency 27, 30
divorce 6
Doctor Who 23, 30

environment 5, 31

family life 5, 6-7, 16, 24-25
fashion 4, 14, 15, 16
films 19, 29, 30
food 4, 9, 10-11, 12, 28, 30

gadgets 6, 20, 21
games 5, 16-17, 18, 28
Greenpeace 5

holidays 10, 24-25
homes 7, 8-9
housework 6
hula hoop 28

immigration 7, 10

meals 10
Moon landing 26, 30
music 4, 21, 22, 23

Pakistan 7
Pong 21
power cuts 4, 30
President Kennedy 26, 30
punishments 12

schools 7, 11, 12-13, 14, 16, 22, 26
Silver Jubilee 27, 30
Smash 11
space hoppers 17
Star Wars 19, 29, 30
strikes 4, 30
supermarkets 11

take-away meals 11
technology 5, 20-21
television 11, 18, 19, 21, 22-23, 26, 30
toys 16-17, 18, 19
Thatcher, Margaret 12, 30

Uganda 7
uniforms 13

video games 21

Walkmans 21
washing 8
watches 20
World Wildlife Fund 5